FINANCIAL FREEDOM

A GUIDE TO CREATE PASSIVE INCOME SOURCE

BLOGRATOR

ISBN 979-888591006-4

"To my family"

Contents

Acknowledgements

I thank my father for teaching me to live life with pride. I thank my mother for teaching me tolerance. I thank my brother for teaching me to be supportive. I thank my wife for teaching me parenting and caring. I thank my son for teaching me to share unconditional love.

ONE

Introduction

In this book I will step by step discuss the total journey form nothing to the way to everything. I will discuss my failed and successful experiments, breakdowns and motivations. In this book I will share all my experiences and knowledge that I acquire during my struggle.

Whatever I will be telling through this book will really matter. This story will give you the knowledge about how money works in internet and in real life. You will learn to create two way earning source, physically and digitally. I will guide you to create maximum flow of income. You will know how to build audience and reach right customers. You will also learn to create digital products and successful ways to sell it.

You have to try to see the things in a way I see it. It will give you the road map to become successful in your life and enjoy the financial freedom. So please read the whole story attentively.

There is no shortcut. If you are looking for quick money and shortcuts then this book can't help you. This book will help you to fix your target. It will help you as a guide. So that you don't repeat the same mistakes like I did. All I know if I would have a guide like this then it would speed up my journey towards financial freedom and save lots of time and money.

Truth is it's all about your involvement and intention how deep you want it. In this path you will face failures, depression and frustrations. You will not get your family by your side to support you. They will think you are wasting your time in computer for hours. You can't make understand about your career goals to your girlfriend or her parents or your family members. If you tell them about your career goals then they will think you crazy. You have to face this question again and again, "How can someone think about anything else except a govt. or private job or business?"

If you still want to choose this life then you are welcome to the world of entrepreneur's.

Let's dig deep into the topic!

TWO

EARLY LIFE

As a kid I wanted to earn from internet using my computer without any investment. I wanted to earn because I needed some extra cash for myself for living my childhood dreams. I wanted to earn without investment because I had no money to invest as a kid. All I had was my father's computer and internet connection.

I was a school student and I loved to read books, not my school books. Every month I used to ask my father to give me money so that I could buy new books. And my father used to fulfill my wish most of the times but he used to ask for bills and the reason of purchase the book.

I didn't get any extra monthly pocket money from my father. My father used to give me two rupees daily when I was nine years old and reading in class five in 2003. The two rupees was for the tiffin break at school so that I can eat something outside.

It was a new school for me and first year I failed in class five. My father didn't scold me for that. He knew I was suffering from headache and was under treatment since a year. Doctor told my father that I couldn't take heavy educational pressures.

I left behind, lost my classmates and became one of the failed senior students of the new batch of class five. Normally students take admission in class five at the age of eleven. I was little early. Though I was considered as one of the failed senior students but still I was one year junior than the most of the new students.

I was in class seven when my father started giving me five rupees a month for school tiffin. In class seven I failed in three subjects in final exam and so that I couldn't make it to next class. I failed in class seven for not taking the study seriously. I used to read story books all the time and play with beyblade toy with friends. This time again my father didn't scold me. He encouraged me to study hard for the next year.

This time my dignity was hurt. I felt how much time I wasted and how fool I was. I could have focused on my studies when I had time.

I promised myself that I would study very hard from then. I truly studied so well that my rank came to 14. I was in class nine when I met a girl and fell in love. It was the first time in my life that I started to focus about my grooming and body language. We used to study together in an English tuition, three days a week. It was 2009 and I was 16.

I was very poor in English grammar before I met the girl. And the girl was our teacher's favourite. I started to focus on English like never before only to impress her.

It was very strange that my crush used to come near me like a magnet. And we used to talk until our teacher would start taking the class. I used to come in tuition even an hour early just to talk with her longer and she would do the same.

I started changing since my first encounter with the girl. Every month I used to approach for new dresses to my father. And I started asking for pocket money from my father. I could manage to convince my father gave me pocket money of rupees 400 INR every month. The day I received the money I spent it all in new dress. My father stopped giving me pocket money from the next month when he found out that I spent it all in a single day for buying new dress. According to my mom I didn't need any new dress that time because I had enough.

But my need was growing day by day. That time some of friends had bikes and where I had an old bicycle since my class five. I wanted to style more to show off in front of that girl that I used to like in my English tuition.

When I completed my secondary exam (10th) and took admission in class eleven with science.

THREE

THE REASON WHY I WANTED TO EARN BADLY

My father never wanted me to study science. He wanted me to study arts and look after his wholesale jewelry business. But I went against my father's decision and chose science. I had a dream about my career. I wanted to study software engineering and become a software engineer. I had deep love with computer subject from my childhood. And after 10th , science was only way to achieve that career I wanted.

My Madhyamik (10+2) exam result wasn't good. Somehow I managed to get first division but the marks weren't good enough for taking science after 10th. My father admitted me in the same school with Arts subjects. But secretly I took admission in different school with science. That school was little far from my home. It would take an hour by bus from my house. Somehow my father came to know about the matter in a month and he understood that he couldn't stop me from taking science. So he managed to transfer me to another school near to my house with science to save my travel time and effort so that I could give more attention to my studies.

My eleventh's study began and I was very excited. For the first three months everything was fine and I was very happy. But then one day my father came home from shop with severe pain in left hand. And after few hours he even couldn't raise his left hand. Because of this pain and weakness in hand he couldn't open shop from the next day. We had a big jewelry shop compare to other jewelry shops in that area with running good numbers of customers. But now it is closed and the daily source of earning stopped.

I, my brother along with my father went to Bangalore for treatment and spent there about 20 days. The doctor whom my father was seeing told father to revisit after 30 days. We came back home and I went back to study. My younger brother started helping my father in business.

But I found out that in my tuitions they have covered two to three chapters during my absence and I was left out. I tried hard to catch the rhythm but it felt difficult to me as in science most of the chapters are connected to each other. Besides I felt very demotivated. Although I tried very hard and almost I was getting back in track. But after 30 days my father went back to Bangalore again for checkup but this time with my brother and the responsibility came to me to open the shop regularly.

In one side there was my love for study and another side was my responsibility as elder son. I chose responsibility. I started going to shop regularly and handled the business.

I used to bring my books to shop but I didn't get time in shop to study because of customers. I used to come home from shop, tired and after that I couldn't get energy to open my books.

I was very depressed. I understood that it is the end of my education and my dreams. My life became very boring. Every day I woke up late in the morning. Then I used to go to my father's jewelry shop, come back at night and then I go to bed.

Like other boys I wanted to go to school and enjoy with friends. After my secondary school I wanted to go to college. I really wanted to experience the lifestyle as a college student. Till then I only read about college in books and watched it in movies. But in class eleven when I understood that I couldn't continue my studies anymore then I became very sad and hopeless. My depression started since then. And yes, I still take antidepressant tablets.

To keep myself engage and feel better I started taking English communication class and I started learning English like never before. In just three months I could speak English.

I took decision that I will drop out this year and restart the education again from the next year. My father and brother came back from Bangalore but still I continue going to shop as usual. My father used to take rest at home. Every day I used to submit the business transaction details to my father. After a few months I told my father that I will drop the year and next year I will resume studying. But my father didn't allow me to do so. He told me to start going to school and I started. But our shop had to close again.

These incidents had an effect in my mind that how a business is completely dependent on one's physical well-being. I started thinking it doesn't matter how hard I work in future if someday I met an accident or some illness and I lose my working capabilities then I will become a financial burden to someone else of my family. So I started searching for a way to earn money where I don't need to be present physically all the time, should be place independent and it should be some kind of automatic process.

After few months when my father was little better then he started going to shop once again. But it was painful for me to see my father going to shop with the heavy bags. I saw him struggling to bring scooty outside of the house as his hand was still weak.

I wanted to earn to support my father. I wanted my father to take rest. Also I wanted to complete my study. So I started looking for some work that shouldn't hamper my study. I was looking for some kind of work from home part time computer based job. I was thinking if I can use my computer and internet to make money then maybe I can find out some way to support my father.

After that I didn't help my father in business as an elder son of the family. Every time I saw my father working hard at this age when people retire from their jobs, I felt guilty. I could kill my dreams and help my father and take over the business entirely and leave my education, life and friends. But I didn't! Because I wanted to take my family to a better position. If I follow the same path like my father then I also have to work for entire life. I wanted to break the custom. I gave myself time to burn. Every time I see my father working hard I became more determined to become a successful person. I was not one of them who waste their time for nothing. I spent hours in learning new things on internet that would help me to become a successful person in future.

I was a last bench student who failed twice in secondary school. It took me long time to memorize my studies. And I was very weak in Maths and English. But despite of all these weaknesses I wanted to learn to earn. Because I knew its money that can pay hospital bills, its money that can help me buy things for my family. And we all will agree in one thing that is our parents deserve better. We want to be felt proud to our parents by achieving a good position in life.

I started doing research on "how to make money from home" so that I could earn and continue my studies together.

There was another incident and reason why I wanted to earn money,

Basically my father doesn't say no if I ask him for money. He asks though what I will do with the money.

It was the time when I was managing my father's business on daily basis for a few months. It was the first time I asked my father to buy me a bike. At first my father promised me that he would buy me a bike. But that week an accident happened in our locality and a teenager died because of rough riding. That incident freaked my parents off and conversion stopped about buying a bike.

Within a few months I again raised the issue that I needed a bike. We went to bike showroom and compared a few bikes. My father wanted me to choose the bike with more mileage so that he could use it for business but I wanted to go for good look.

This duel went on for a few more months and my father didn't purchase any bike and I became very angry. After that I promised my father I would never ask him for a bike again. I also told him that I would buy a bike of my own choice by myself with my one month's earning one day.

My father told me to earn 200 rupees first

After hearing my pledge, my father told me to learn how to earn 200 INR a month first. That sentence from my father hit me in my head and I still remember the sentence. It was true I didn't know how to earn money. Earning money is kind of a technique. The more you are skilled the technique the more you can earn.

I believe getting a fixed salary in a month isn't the money making skill. It's the businessmen doesn't matter small of big they actually know the art of earning. I started thinking how I can start earning money by myself. I started thinking about what skills I have. I had no money so that I can't invest in any reselling business. So I had to focus on giving service. I was a student of class eleven and English was my favorite subject. I decided to start teaching English.

FOUR

I STARTED LOOKING FOR WAYS TO EARN MONEY

It all started when I was about to 18 years old. I was looking for a way to earn money using the computer and internet. I started doing research about it and found many websites that was providing work from home computer based job but with a subscription fee.

I didn't have any bank account that time so I never paid any website. But one website was giving cash on delivery service. And the subscription fee was too low, around 300 INR (less than 5 USD). So I applied for the work. In seven days a package reached my home. I found activation link, username and password inside it. With excitement I opened the website and logged in.

It was something like copy paste work. There was a referral link that I needed to paste in social media and another web platforms so that more people get registered with the job like I did and this way I would get paid 100 rupee for each successful referral. I worked for first few days but slowly I realized that I have become a fool and the company wants me to fool more people. This wasn't kind of work I was looking for. This was some kind of work that cheats people. Then I checked about the company's background and saw so many people have registered complain against the company because the company never paid the customers. Whether the company would pay me or not, I couldn't let people fall into the same trap. So I stopped the process.

I understood that on internet some people have opened their business to sell their service to the desperate people like me. But I never stopped doing research to get the right way to make money from internet. Because deep down I knew there must be some true way and I didn't lose hope and keep researching.

There was another idea that I tried and failed.

You may have heard about the term chain marketing or money marketing. It's like you join under someone and you have to join two more people under you. The more people you will join under you the more money you can earn. They will tell you this way you can earn lakhs of rupees in a month. They will show you some pictures of celebrities or ministers who are the brand ambassador or representing the company.

I was totally convinced by an agent of the company whom I met in my English Communication class. As I had no real life money making experience before so very easily I fell in his prey as I was also desperate to make lot of money.

But to join the company I needed to purchase any products above 1500 INR. Therefore I started asking for money to my father. But my father refused to give me the money and told me to focus on studies. Then I started convincing my mother for the money so that I can join the company. After trying for few days my mother was convinced when I told her that I will return the money once I earn it from the company.

I purchased a product worth rupees 1500 INR and joined the company. After joining the company I started taking training from them every weekend. The training was all about "how to convince more people to join the company and the superiority of the products of the company." In few days I started feeling wrong about the total idea. It's like begging to people so that they join the company and buy their daily products from us. I had little ego problem from my childhood. And begging to people wasn't my thing.

Though I tried to convince few people I know but I failed. I even made some drawings and flowcharts but nothing worked! In few months I left hope and stopped working on behalf of the company.

So I went back to my computer and internet. I did really good research and study and finally I realized that money can be made from internet in the following ways,

1. Blogging (Affiliate Marketing and Google Adsense).
2. Affiliate Marketing (Can be done from a website and YouTube channel).
3. Self Publishing.
4. YouTube Channel (Google Ads and Affiliate Marketing).

I understood that I needed a website. But I had no clue how to build a website. I used to think I must be an expert to create a website myself. I knew I had no money to hire an expert for it. I did research on internet about "how to create a website?" I got some solution but it was costly for me to run a website. So I started looking for "how to create a website for free?"

I found that from WordPress I can create a free website. I opened a free WordPress account and opened a free website. My first free WordPress website is still roaming around the internet.

After a few days I understood that the free website comes with limitations. I can't apply for adsense ads with a free wordpress website. Though I can do affiliate marketing. I opened Amazon affiliate account and started posting affiliate links from my account with free content from amazon. But something wasn't right. I was doing all wrong. What was missing was experience and knowledge. There are a few questions to consider are as follows,

1. How people will know you have a website?
2. Why people will trust a free website? (A free website is always a sub domain)
3. Why your free or paid website will come in google search ranking?
4. If you share your website link in social media pages and groups then what is there in your website that will convert the visitors into customers?
5. What are you selling?
6. If you think more visitors will give you good earning from google ads then forget it (If you are running a paid website).

When someone is just a beginner in this field then this kind of very silly ideas will come like me. I was too far from the reality. But I was solving my problems one by one. I decided to buy a domain and run my own website. For that reason I started learning HTML and CSS from YouTube. But I had no earning source to buy and run the website. It was a new business idea and I needed investment. My father never trusted my business ideas so I couldn't get continuous funding to run my experiments.

I understood that I needed a source of income so that I can fund my experiments myself. So I decided that I will open a tutorial center at my home. I put a sign board outside my house and gave my tutorial center the name "YST Tutorial Home"

FIVE

I STARTED TEACHING TO FUND MY EXPERIMENTS

At the end of 2011 I started my tutorial home. I was very weak student in English but since 2009 I became very interested about English Grammar and English became my favourite language. I started discovering the grammar by myself. I started purchasing English grammar books of different writers. In 2011 I took English communication class and within three months I could speak English. I found out that I was quite good in explaining English grammar to my friends. So I decided to start teaching English grammar as a private tutor. I started with five students for free who were in the same class of mine and very weak in English. It was my first experiment to testify my theory that whether I could teach English. My five students performed very well in exam and one of the students got the highest marks in the school in the final exam. In a year I became very famous in my locality for English teaching. I was making around 10K INR a month. I created my own formula for English grammar to teach the weak students. Even I rented a house for only teaching. I remember teaching around 40 students that time. I totally forgot about my dream to make money from internet and become rich. But God reminds me! It was going very good since one day I fell very sick and was admitted to the hospital. Doctor told it was Jaundice and the level was very high. I was earning enough money and I had rented a house for teaching. I was only 18 that time. Most of the time I used to eat street food. I started spending my money on my girlfriend and friends. I was living my life with freedom.

I used to go my home to sleep only. Because of Jaundice I was admitted to the hospital for almost a week. I was so weak that I couldn't even walk 20 steps. I was in complete bed rest. It took almost one and half of the month to get my strength back. At the time of my sickness I realized that it was only the family who was there by my side in my bad time, not friends or girlfriend. After the recovery I realized that I have lost my source of earning. I had no students left. My one year struggle went in vain. This incident again reminded me that it doesn't matter how successful you are but if your money coming from the source that depends on your physical ability then it has to fall one day. That's why smart people invest their money in such places to create passive income source and money flow for lifetime. Although I lost my earning source but I restarted teaching again. This time I advertised in local newspaper and hung banners in front of some schools. Also I hired a leaflet boy to distribute leaflets in front of schools. I started getting students again. My teaching went on in same pattern. I was teaching English subject to school students for 200 INR a month. During this time I didn't study my science subjects seriously. I wanted to study the eleven class again as I couldn't do it properly. But my father discussed with the head master and suggested me not to drop out in eleven instead they suggested if needed then I should restudy the 12th class. I didn't sit for my eleventh exam but I was promoted to class twelve. I was busy from morning to night for my teaching work. All of my batches were full. I didn't get time for my self-study. Next year when it was time for final exam then I dropped out and decided to restudy the 12th class again. Next year I minimized my batches and started going to school regularly. I remember only for a few months I took my science tuition classes but wasn't satisfied with the teaching. It felt like my precious time was being wasted. Instead of taking tuition classes I started studying all the science subjects by myself. I was very regular to school. I used to study my books in school during free classes. I used to take my school classes very attentively. So instead of two years I completed my 10+2 in three years. All my school friends were already in college one year ago. I used to go to school in school uniform when my friends used to go to college in casual dress. It was a prestige issue for me. Even my brother was studying in same class of mine. Both of us completed higher secondary education in the same year of 2013. Only I know how tough I had to be inside to face the situation among the family members, society and friends. I could ignore all these because still the dream was live inside me that one day I will go to college and complete my study in software engineering and become a software engineer. I remember during my higher secondary exam also I didn't stop teaching. The exam result came out and I could only achieve 50%. I was happy because at last I don't have to take the huge pressure of science again. My first target to achieve my dream goal was complete. Now I moved to my second target that was studying software engineering. I gave joint entrance exam but couldn't get a qualify rank. So I was looking for direct admission in any engineering college. But after doing research about the college fees it was too much for me. I didn't want to pressurize my father to fulfill my dream career. I was convinced by a senior about taking BCA instead of B.Tech in software engineering. The senior was doing MCA from Kolkata and who was also a student of Malda college. He told me there is no big difference in B.Tech in software engineering and BCA. Even some students go for MCA after B.Tech. He also told me that BCA and MCA are mostly focused of programming languages. Whether it is BCA or B.Tech I will get similar career opportunity in IT sector. There in three years I have to study 36 different subject that is 6 subjects in every semester. Also I came to know that the education fee is quite less in Malda College that is 25k per year. I came to know that arts students can also take admission in BCA if they have computer application subject in eleven and twelve. In my school I couldn't take computer application as my forth subject during higher secondary because in class nine and ten I didn't have computer in my optional subject. I wanted to take computer in optional subject in nine and ten but it was my father's and teacher's decision not to take it as it will give me extra burden in Madhyamik exam. I believe everything happens for a good reason. I took admission in Malda College with BCA. It felt like my long wanted dream came true. I was so happy. Computer was my love from my childhood but for some reasons I was always separated from the subject earlier. I didn't take any teacher, I started studying myself. I bought all the books of my syllabus. The college was same as my dream college. Our department had a library with lot of computer books. The library was center of my attraction. In first and second semester I got highest marks in final exam. My attendance was 97%. I was making average 13,000 Indian rupees in a month from teaching this time. To earn 13k I had to invest my most of the time in teaching. I almost forgot that my ultimate goal was to make a passive source. I also noticed that how hard I tried but I could not increase my earning from 13k. And to earn that money I had to involve all of myself mentally and physically. That's how most people got stuck in earning and forgot about the real dreams. I call it "MAYA". Maya is the attachment with everything around us. I understood that I was going wrong way. Making 13k a month wasn't my goal. I wanted financial freedom. I wanted to get out of work and money gravity by playing smart. And I need to do to as fast as possible. If I can't figure out how to make money without working for it then I will die working like other normal people. This is a kind of financial education that we all need to get out of the "money & work gravity." I really left teaching and came to zero from 13k. I took this decision to clear my mind from everything. So that I can rethink what I am doing and which way I am going. I started asking for money from my father and brother. My younger brother got always money as he was seeing our family business. I remember those days when I started asking for 20 rupees everyday from my mom in the evening. Every evening I used to go out with my girlfriend and we used to spend 20 rupees in "MOMO". Momo is Indian street food. It's very cheap and popular. I didn't like momo at all because it was on news that they mix ajinomoto in momos to make it tasty. Ajinomoto isn't good for health according to news. But I had to eat it because of my girlfriend. I tried to convince her to try different food sometimes but she only liked momo. So I had to eat it too. Oh, I forgot to tell about my girlfriends. Do you remember I was taking English communication class once? I had a girlfriend from that class but I broke up before my higher secondary exam. I was single when I took admission in college and within a few months I got a girlfriend. She was my classmate. But the relationship worked for one year only. Luckily in second year I met another girl who was my junior. We came in relationship and that worked for 3.5 years till 2018. Let's come back to the topic. After I stopped teaching eventually I lost my source of my earning. Most of the time when we go out my girlfriend had to spend and everyday in the evening we used to go out. In a month or two my girlfriend found it irritating. One day she said it all. She told me, "Every time I got to check my purse before going out with you. What I will tell my parents whom I am meeting with? What is his source of earning?..." Till I had money in my pocket she had no issues with me. I understood her opinion though. But I felt very humiliated. I never had these feelings that I had to listen. I couldn't make her understand that I stopped making money to upgrade myself. I started working hard at home in my computer. I started to spend almost 12 to 14 hours with my computer. In few months I got unbearable back pain below my neck. During this time I started learning a lot of things that really helped me in future. That I have discussed in my book.

I was very weak student in English but since 2009 I became very interested about English Grammar and English became my favourite language. I started purchasing English grammar books of different writers. In 2011 I took English communication class and within three months I could speak English.

I found out that I was quite good in explaining English grammar to my friends.

So I decided to start teaching English grammar as a private tutor. I started with five students for free who were in the same class of mine and very weak in English. It was my first experiment to testify my theory that whether I could teach English. My five students performed very well in exam and one of the students got the highest marks in the school in the final exam.

In a year I became very famous in my locality for English teaching. I was making around 10K INR a month. I created my own formula for English grammar to teach the weak students. Even I rented a house for only teaching. I remember teaching around 40 students that time. I totally forgot about my dream to make money from internet and become rich. But God reminds me!

It was going very good since one day I fell very sick and was admitted to the hospital. Doctor told it was Jaundice and the level was very high.

I was earning enough money and I had rented a house for teaching. I was only 18 that time. Most of the time I used to eat street foods. I started spending my money on my girlfriend and friends. I was living my life with freedom. I used to go my home to sleep only.

Because of Jaundice I was admitted to the hospital for almost a week. I was so weak that I couldn't even walk 20 steps. I was in complete bed rest. It took almost one and half of the month to get my strength back. At the time of my sickness I realized that it was only the family who was there by my side in my bad time, not friends or girlfriend.

After the recovery I realized that I have lost my source of earning. I had no students left. My one year struggle went in vain.

This incident again reminded me that it doesn't matter how successful you are but if your money coming from the source that depends on your physical ability then it has to fall one day. That's why smart people invest their money in such places to create passive income source and money flow for lifetime.

Although I lost my earning source but I restarted teaching again. This time I advertised in local newspaper and hung banners in front of some schools. Also I hired a leaflet boy to distribute leaflets in front of schools. I started getting students again.

My teaching went on in same pattern. I was teaching English subject to school students for 200 INR a month.

During this time I didn't study my science subjects seriously. I wanted to study the eleven class again as I couldn't do it properly. But my father discussed about it with the head master. He suggested my father it will be better if I don't dropout in 11. Because they will pass everyone in class twelve and if needed then I should restudy the 12th class. I didn't sit for my eleventh exam but was promoted to class twelve.

I was busy from morning to night for my teaching work. All of my batches were full. I didn't get time for my self-study.

Next year when it was time for final exam then I decided not to sit for exam as I didn't study properly. I wanted to study class XII again from the beginning.

Next year I minimized my batches and started going to school regularly. I remember only for a few months I took my science tuition classes but wasn't satisfied with the teaching. It felt like my precious time was being wasted. Instead of taking tuition classes I started studying all the science subjects by myself. I was very regular to school. I used to study my books in school during free classes. I used to take my school classes very attentively.

So instead of two years I completed my 10+2 in three years. All my school friends were already in college one year ago. I used to go to school in school uniform when my friends used to go to college in casual dress. It was a prestige issue for me. Even my brother was studying in same class of mine. Both of us completed higher secondary education in the same year of 2013.

Only I know how tough I had to be inside to face the situation among the family members, society and friends. I could ignore all these because still the dream was live inside me that one day I will go to college and complete my study in software engineering and become a software engineer.

I remember during my higher secondary exam also I didn't stop teaching. The exam result came out and I could only achieve 50%. I was happy because at last I don't have to take the huge pressure of science again.

My first target to achieve my dream goal was complete. Now I moved to my second target that was studying software engineering. I gave joint entrance exam but couldn't get a qualify rank. So I was looking for direct admission in any engineering college. But after doing research about the college fees it was too much for me. I didn't want to pressurize my father to fulfill my dream career.

I was convinced by a senior about taking BCA instead of B.Tech in software engineering. The senior was doing MCA from Kolkata and who was also a student of ABC College. He told me there is no big difference in B.Tech in software engineering and BCA. Even some students go for MCA after B.Tech. He also told me that BCA and MCA are mostly focused of programming languages. Whether it is BCA or B.Tech I will get similar career opportunity in IT sector. There in three years I have to study 36 different subjects that is 6 subjects in every semester. Also I came to know that the education fee is quite less in ABC College that is 25k per year.

I came to know that arts students can also take admission in BCA if they have computer application subject in eleven and twelve.

In my school I couldn't take computer application as my forth subject during higher secondary because in class nine and ten I didn't have computer in my optional subject. I wanted to take computer in optional subject in nine and ten but it was my father's and teacher's decision not to take it as it will give me extra burden in Madhyamik exam.

I believe everything happens for a good reason. I took admission in ABC College with BCA. It felt like my long wanted dream came true. I was so happy. Computer was my love from my childhood but for some reasons I was always separated from the subject earlier. I didn't take any teacher, I started studying myself. I bought all the books of my syllabus. The college was same as my dream college. Our department had a library with lot of computer books. The library was center of my attraction. In first and second semester I got highest marks in final exam. My attendance was 97%.

I was making average 13,000 Indian rupees in a month from teaching this time. To earn 13k I had to invest my most of the time in teaching. I almost forgot that my ultimate goal was to make a passive source. I also noticed that how hard I tried but I could not increase my earning from 13k. And to earn that money I had to involve all of myself mentally and physically. That's how most people got stuck in earning and forgot about the real dreams. I call it "MAYA". Maya is the attachment with everything around us.

I understood that I was going wrong way. Making 13k a month wasn't my goal. I wanted financial freedom. I wanted to get out of work and money gravity by playing smart. And I need to do to as fast as possible. If I can't figure out how to make money without working for it then I will die working like other normal people. This is a kind of financial education that we all need to get out of the "money & work gravity."

I really left teaching and came to zero from 13k. I took this decision to clear my mind from everything. So that I can rethink what I am doing and which way I am going.

I started asking for money from my father and brother. My younger brother got always money as he was seeing our family business.

I remember those days when I started asking for 20 rupees everyday from my mom in the evening. Every evening I used to go out with my girlfriend and we used to spend 20 rupees in "MOMO". Momo is Indian street food. It's very cheap and popular. I didn't like momo at all because it was on news that they mix ajinomoto in momos to make it tasty. Ajinomoto isn't good for health according to news. But I had to eat it because of my girlfriend. I tried to convince her to try different food sometimes but she only liked momo. So I had to eat it too.

Oh, I forgot to tell about my girlfriends. Do you remember I was taking English communication class once? I had a girlfriend from that class but I broke up before my higher secondary exam. I was single when I took admission in college and within a few months I got a girlfriend. She was my classmate. But the relationship worked for one year only. Luckily in second year I met another girl who was my junior. We came in relationship and that worked for 3.5 years till 2018.

Let's come back to the topic. After I stopped teaching eventually I lost my source of my earning. Most of the time when we go out with my girlfriend had to spend and everyday in the evening we used to go out. In a month or two my girlfriend found it irritating. One day she said it all. She told me, "Every time I got to check my purse before going out with you. What I will tell my parents whom I am meeting with? What is his source of earning?..."

Till I had money in my pocket she had no issues with me. I understood her opinion though. But I felt very humiliated. I never had these feelings that I had to listen. I couldn't make her understand that I stopped making money to upgrade myself.

I started working hard at home in my computer. I started to spend almost 12 to 14 hours with my computer. In few months I got unbearable back pain below my neck.

During this time I started learning a lot of things that really helped me in future. That I have discussed in my book.

SIX

WHAT KIND OF CAREER A MIDDLE CLASS INDIAN PARENTS WANT FOR THEIR CHILDREN?

I was in 10th standard when I told my father that I didn't want a government job. After hearing this father took me to a psychiatrist for counseling.

I could never make my parents understand my intentions about my career. And that's why my father never wanted to invest on my ideas. So whatever I needed to do I had to do of my own.

I am from a middle class Indian family where we are always taught to kill our dreams and follow what other people is doing. My mom would always say "See what your uncle's son is doing why you don't follow him?" And my father would say, "See, the other businessmen's sons are managing the store. Why can't you learn from them?"

My question to my and other parents who tell their children to follow someone else is why do you want to see a copy of someone else in your children? Your children may have some qualities better than them. Why don't you tell your children to be like Sundar Pichai or Mark Zuckerberg or Bill Gates who are also successful?

But no our parents will never tell us to follow them because we are from middle class family and we can't see big dreams.

Over these kinds of topic I used to fight with my father and could never win from him. I believe my problem back then was the problem of most of the poor and middle class family's children who want to see and live their dreams.

Indian parents want their children to get a government job to settle down in life. People consider that government job is the most secure job for life. Once you enter into the job and stays with it for lifetime. Here people believe job in private sector has no security. And that's why bride's parents always look for a groom with a government job. Parents tell their children from their childhood that they need to get a government job any how to survive in the society.

But preparing for government job and getting it is not an easy here. After completing your education you have to prepare for competitive exam if you want to crack government job exam.

Preparing for competitive exam is not cheap if you are taking it from any institute.

If you want to be a teacher of primary school then after HS you besides competitive exam preparation you have to study D. El. Ed.) from a government or private college. The Diploma in Elementary Education (D. EI. Ed) is a two year professional programme of teacher education. It aims to prepare teacher for the elementary stage of education, i.e. classes I to VIII.

And if you want to be a high school teacher then after graduation besides competitive exam preparation you have to complete your B. ED degree. It is also a two year study programme.

Whether it is D.El.ED or B.ED the study cost is also not cheap.

If you are thinking after all this a person gets a ticket for government job then you are thinking wrong. Even if you crack the exam in few years of trying by luck then paper leaks and Court cases will be stopping the recruitment process for next few years. And very few people are lucky enough to get the government job without ....

My whole point is why giving so many years behind education when we all know we are doing it to earn money at the end of the day. When I was in secondary school then I used to study everything else except my syllabus books. Before a month of exam it felt like torture when I had to study the information that I didn't want to know.

I liked to read books very much since my childhood. Knowing something new was always a hobby to me. When I started earning money myself since then I started collecting books I like. I have full room of books and I am still collecting more.

Knowledge should be free and it should be us who will decide what we want to study and what to not. The system can't force us to study the information that we don't need to know. If a teenager wants to know about physics deeply and bought some books on it or love to read Albert Einstein's, Stephen Hawking's books over his boring syllabus book they what's wrong with it?

To get the financial freedom we need educational freedom first. Some piece of paper can't decide our qualification and depth of knowledge.

I know you won't get support from your loved ones emotionally, mentally and financially if you want to walk against the system to live your dreams.

But I did!

I never attempt for a government exam. I remember one incident when my brother applied for a government exam. It was on Sunday. The exam place was given 30+ KM away from our house. I decided to go with my brother to the exam place. I saw all the buses were full people were hanging behind the bus. Some people are sitting over top of the bus. There are all going for government exam. If 10 vacancies are there then 10,000 or more people are applying for it. Besides government exam is not free you have to pay exam fees to attempt the exam.

On the other hand private sector jobs are very easy to get. All you need to do is to work on your English communication skills and basic computer knowledge and you are good to go. The more you develop your industry standard skills the better position you deserve in a private sector also it requires time and experience. Besides you don't need to pay a single rupee to anyone to get a job in private sector if you are a deserving candidate.

SEVEN

Normal VS Professional Internet Users

How Normal user Use Internet

Content is the real king of internet. Content in internet are mainly created with image, video and text.

We the normal internet users use internet for two purposes,

1. Fun.
2. Information gathering and learning.

People do lots of Google searches to get solutions in their daily life. Google's artificial intelligence system keeps tracking websites and information in the internet ocean. Once any user searches anything in Google's search engine, it matches the web pages that contains most relevant information with the search keywords and gives the search results to the user. According to me 70 to 80 percent information we access in the internet are free.

We also spend our time on internet for fun. The apps and websites we use are mostly for free. We can't survive with normal text message and call app in our smart phone like before.

But how come we don't need to pay for most of the services that we use and spend most of our time in a day? If we use the app for free then what the website/app owners make out of it? And how they are becoming richer day by day?

Okay! Let me explain. We all use most of the apps/websites like shopping, social media, movie, video, music, games and dating, right?

And we use it for free unless we want to go for paid option for more features. In most popular apps when you use a free platform then you are forced to see ads.

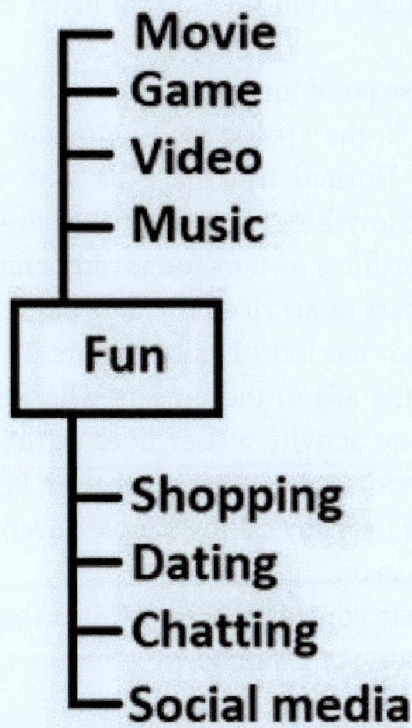

Here is a story.

Once upon a time there were a big pond where the pond owner offered free food and living. Knowing this so many fishes started to move to the pond and started living happily without paying for foods and room rents. The pond owner gave a room to the each of the fishes and free foods every day. In few days more fishes came to know about the place with free food and living and they moved to the pond.

But there was a condition of the pond. If any fish would be caught by fishing by any other fish then the fish had to pay .5 USD to the other fish who would do the fishing. And after paying the .5 USD the caught fish can return to the pond.

In few months the fishes of the pond became so lazy and habituated of the free food and comfort.

One day the pond owner advertised that he got a "Good place for unlimited fishing at 10 USD/day." The rich fishes started booking for fishing at the pond. And they started catching lots of fishes from the pond.

But there were never lack of fishes in the pond because everyone wanted the free food and living.

Moral of the story:

1.Pond owner make lots of money from the rich fishes.

2.Rich fishes make money from the normal fishes they catch from the pond.

3. The **normal fishes** use pond for free.

Here the pond owner is the app or website owner who is giving free services in the internet. Normal fishes are us who are using the free platforms without paying anything. The rich fishes are the business men, companies who pay the platform owners for advertisement.

Basically business owners or service providers pay for advertisement in a free popular platform that has lots of daily visitors. The advertise method work as filters. It shows the ads to those users who actually relate to the advertisement. Because any activity a user does in the free platform, the platform records the behavior and interest of the user. Besides the platforms keeps the basic data of the users by asking simple questions like name, age, gender, favorite color and so on.

The advertisers get basic control of the platform that which users they want to target with their ads. For example,

1. Which gender?
2. Which location?
3. Age between?
4. Field for interest (e.g., shopping, dating, food, music, movie, school, college and so on)

Besides the platform's AI system also helps the advertise to reach the right audience so that the advertisers get relevant customers from the platform.

If the advertisers can't make profit from the advertisement money then the advertisers won't repeat the advertisement. So the advertisers profit is very important to the platform owners.

This way the free apps and websites work. And we the normal users are the product.

How the Professionals/Creators Use Internet?

Creators create content for internet. Content can be text, image and video. We know the most popular platform for video content that is YouTube. And most popular text content we can say Wikipedia. But any other websites and app can provide text, image and video content for free or paid for the normal internet users. The reason creators create content for internet is they can earn money from the creativity. Internet is an ocean where huge amount of world population come on a daily basis. Any country's users can access information from any country's website through search result or direct address (like www.).

As the distance doesn't cost a penny extra in internet so the whole world is like in a single room. People can sell anything anywhere. Beside physical products it can be digital products or services also. A digital product doesn't need any physical activities to reach to the other user. It can go in a second with a single click on purchase button. A digital product can be an online course, an image, an article, software, game, music, and movie and so on.

Creators can feed the internet with their creativity any time. It isn't like 9 to 5 job. A creator can do 9 to 5 job and after that he can spend two hours for creative work. Those works are same as investments because after few months or years it starts generating money. This money is called **"The passive source of income."**

This income is your retire plan from your daily job or business. Because once you find the way to create the source of your passive income then in no time the income can generate more money than your salary.

Creators make money from Adsense ads:

We are habituate to use free services on internet. And those free platforms get lots of daily traffic worldwide. That is why any free platform with lots of traffic is the best place for advertisement.

YouTube is the most popular and biggest video platform in the world.

From any normal user to big company can pay Google for advertisement on YouTube using Google Adwords. YouTube pays 60 percent of its advertising revenue to the creators/ channel owners once the channel is eligible for YouTube partner program. That is that channel owner can monetize it's videos on YouTube i.e., viewers will see ads in the videos of the channel. And this way the channel owners can make money from YouTube.

In 2018 YouTube made some strict rules for all the creators. All YouTube channels must have 4000 hours watch time and 1000 new subscribers within last 12 months to be eligible for YouTube partner program to make money from YouTube.

Google has Adsense ads for content program for the website owners. That is the visitors in the website will see advertisement and the website owner will get ad revenue from Google.

Also there is Google Admob program for the android app owners. We see ads in the apps that we use in our android phone and the app owners get ad revenue from Google.

All three programs YouTube partner program, Adsense for content program and Admob program will be connected to one single place that is

Google Adsense. All the earnings from three platforms for last 28 days gather in the Adsense account. Once the Adsense account reaches the threshold limit that is 100 USD then the money gets transferred to the Adsense owner's bank account.

How business owner use Internet?

We can use internet for free at the condition that we have to see the ads.

Facebook own Whatsapp and Instagram. For now business owners or service providers can use facebook and Instagram for advertisement. In Facebook the user needs to create a page that will be linked to the user's profile. The page owner will get boost option in any post that will be eligible for boost. Also the page owner can boost the page for more like or click on the button. In Instagram the user needs to switch to business account in order to use the advertisement service. In Facebook there is Facebook Ad manager page and mobile app to control and monitor the ads, payments and statistics.

The process is very simple "same thing again and again"

Your daily routine should be

1. A YouTube video,
2. An article for your blog,
3. Your daily work on a digital product.

EIGHT

HOW TO START AN ONLINE BUSINESS AND MAKE MONEY?

Any business with investments speeds up very quickly if you have good management plans where business without investments may take little longer to generate revenues. But both of the ways can be very successful depending on business plan and marketing strategy.

To become a successful business you need an accurate long run plan, good focus, dedication, hardworking, honesty, flexibility, investments(of time, money, man power, good will etc) and proper knowledge on the field.

Basic questions that may come to your mind when you think to start a online business:

- What will be the online business?
- How to start an online business?
- How to get customers online?
- Why customers will buy products/services online from me when there are popular platforms available?
- How to accept payments and orders from customer?
- How to deliver the products to the customers?

Well, I will answer all of the above mentioned questions in this article. There will be two main segments for every point these are,

1. How to start an online business without investment?
2. How to start an online business with investment?

#1 What will be the online business?

If you are a newbie then this question is very common for you like other newbies. I will clear your concept about starting an online business here. Online business can be something that can be sold whether it is physical or digital.

Examples of physical products:

Toys, dresses, ornaments, gift items, bags and others.

Example of digital products:

Selling pictures (photography), selling articles, online teaching service, graphic design and other services.

You can buy the physical products from the local or online wholesale market. So if you want to start with selling physical products then you need to invest on your business whether you buy a single or dozen of items to sell first. People get confused about choosing an item category to start a business with. For the starter it is a test ride. So one starter should always start with a single type of category with small investment.

For example: Supposed you have decided to sell smartphone back covers. Then you have to do good research on the current market and demand very closely. Also you have to keep your eye on the new released smartphones. Nobody will tell you the secrets of a business. It must be you to go through the small experiments. Also you have to be smart enough to discover the secrets of a business from the business persons you are dealing with.

But if you got some talents like writing skills, photoshop, photography, animation, web design, singing and others then you can start your online business without investing on physical products. You can turn your skills into digital products and sell them using a free or paid platform.

For example, when you start reading an article or news on internet then basically you get attracted not only by the headline but also the picture. A creative photography or edited picture has a strong potential to grab the attention of a reader. That's why a good graphic designer is on hot demand to the content creators. You can also sell your edited creative picture as an eBook or paperback book cover.

Whether you want to sell any physical or digital product/service you need a platform that is called a website. But you can't do that with just a website. You will need an e-Commerce website where people can place an order and payment. You will need a management software installed on your website. If you are unaware of the idea how can you get an e-Commerce site to start your business then the problem can be solved in two ways,

1. Either ***you hire a web designer.*** or,
2. ***Learn how to create an e-commerce website***.

Also there are free ways to start selling,

1. From a free website - selling physical or digital product/service both possible.
2. Using a freelancing platform - Only possible for selling digital product/service.

#2 How to start an online business?

Basically to start an online business you need a platform free or paid.

Talking about paid:

If you are ready to invest on business then you can hire professionals for that. Like if you want to sell cloths online then you need to hire a web-designer first to create the e-commerce platform. You will need to buy a professional theme and some premium plugins according to the web designer to give your website a professional look. Then you need to buy clothes for men, women and children from local or online wholesale markets or contact brands for that. Then you will need a photographer + photo editor who will capture the pictures of the dresses and edit them. After that the web designer will list your products on your e-commerce website. Next you will need to incorporate your business under Ministry of Corporate Affairs (for India) as you will sell your products in different states of your country. There are companies who provide the service where you can incorporate your business. It's better to know about the laws of your country. So you need to consult with a lawyer for that. After that you will contact the companies who will give you the payment gateway facilities that you can integrate in your website to accept payments from customers. Also you need SEO analyst, digital marketing specialist and content developers to bring customers to your website.

Talking about free:

Option 1: You can open a free blog/website (Click here To know how to get a free website).

Using a free website it is possible to sell physical or digital product. But there will be so many limitations. Besides you can't own the trust of your customer and become a brand. So it will be almost free if you buy a domain and hosting yourself and start selling your skills.

Option 2: You can search for popular freelancing platforms that suit you. There you can sell your skills as gigs and send proposal for works that you can do. You will get so many traffics related to your skills. And it is better free option than having a free or paid website. Once you get established there then your will have money to invest on your online business ideas.

#3 How to get customers online?

This is the most important topic for any online/offline business. Here you need to educate yourself about some technical topics or hire the experts.

You need to educate yourself on the topics like **SEO friendly content development, SEO Techniques and digital marketing (email, social-media, search engine marketing etc).**

I have discussed on this topic in details here ***https://blogratorofficial.blogspot.in/2018/02/how-to-make-money-from-blog.html***

 # 4 Why the visitors will buy products/services online from me when there are popular platforms available?

You must know how to become a familiar face or brand. Consider a YouTuber who has thousands of subscribers who blindly follow him. So it will become very easy if he recommends a T-shirt or any product to his subscribers that he sells. For example I love to watch popular YouTuber Casey Neistat who recently started selling his own T-shirt from his website https://shopcaseyneistat.com/

There are also other options available like technical parts that relates to the previous question. Please follow the link from the previous question where I have given every possible detail.

 # 5 How to accept payments and orders from customer?

You need to integrate online payment gateway in your website. If you are using e-commerce platform then it will be very easy by installing some plugins. But you must have accounts at the payment gateway service providers like *paypal*(to receive from individuals), *payoneer*(to receive from international companies) and others. Like in India there are some national payment gateway service providers if you sell inside the country but for international customers paypal will be needed.

NINE

Blogging - Web Hosting - Digital Marketing - SEO

What is a blog?

A blog is a kind of a website where we share our knowledge, emotions and experiences through writing. Basically a blog can be easily maintained with popular CMS applications like WordPress, Blogger, Joomla, Tumblr, Quota etc. CMS stands for Content Management System. These web applications manage the contents that we publish in our blog. The best part is we don't need to learn any coding to run the blog on CMS platform.

These CMS applications can be classified into two categories, Open source and closed source. The open source CMS web applications can be installed on any web hosting servers that we purchase to host our personal domain.

All the above mentioned CMS application providers provide users free space* and unique sub domains of user's choice to start a free blog.

What are the types of blogs?

You can't force yourself to write an article in your blog. Blogging comes automatically when you feel like expressing your feelings from your heart. So before you start a blog you should be aware of the types of blogs and its future. According to my observation I have categorized blogs into two main parts Personal/Lifestyle blog and Niche blog.

Personal/Lifestyle blog

It is a type of blog where people write and share their personal experience, story and emotion. You can write whatever you want on any topic. There are no rules to follow. It will help you to find people like you on internet. It is something like sharing status, experience, emotions, pictures and videos in social media. But social media don't give you money for all that activity, creativity and sharing. Also you got many limitations on social media to express your creativity properly. That's why you need a blog or website.

Niche blog

Niche blog is something when your whole blog and writing is on a particular topic. It is one of the most popular options that people choose to make money from blogging. Basically through their writing the bloggers recommend third party products or services. Those are called affiliate products and services and sold by different owners/website. Niche bloggers use the links of the products/services with their unique tracking code. And whenever a visitor makes a purchase from the links then the blogger gets commission from the owner/website. The commissions can be 8 to 80 percent of the product price. One of the biggest trustworthy affiliate service provider companies is Amazon. Also there are so many like Commission Junction, Click Bank, ShareaSale etc.

Examples of niche blogs:

There can be more than hundreds of niche for example Health & Wellness, Fashion & Style, Makeup & Beauty, Pets, Travel, Exercise & Fitness, Gardening and so on.

Popular free Blogging platforms depending on blog types:

WordPress.com:

WordPress.com helps you to grow your audience and community from inside WordPress besides google search and social media sharing. But it is not a good option to start a free Personal/Lifestyle blogging here. Because if you want to monetize your blog under Google AdSense for Content to make money and you are using free option in WordPress then you can't do it. To monetize your blog under AdSense for Content you have to upgrade to premium plan and that starts at 96 USD/year (no monthly payment option). Where other popular hosting services provide much better facilities in less than 60 USD/year and also you get monthly payment options.

But if your target is niche blogging then wordpress may be a good option for you. Because you can earn from affiliate marketing with the free plan. But lots of AdSense ads of WordPress will definitely move your traffic in different direction. To remove the AdSense ads of WordPress again you have to pay yearly 48 USD. Besides you got no control over the emails of your subscribers.

Blogger:

Blogger was developed by Pyra Labs, which was bought by Google in 2003. Generally, the blogs are hosted by Google at a subdomain of blogspot.com. Blogger cannot be installed on a web server as it is not open source.

If you start a free blog on "Blogger" then you will be benefited in every way whether you start a Personal/Lifestyle blog or Niche blog. Because blogger is owned by Google and Google won't put their ads on your blog. Also you can apply for AdSense for Content program in your free blog when your blog will be eligible. And also you can buy and link your personal domain in your free blog in affordable price. As you know people make money for uploading videos on YouTube and they don't have to pay extra penny like that people can make money from free blogs in Blogger.

Paid platforms for blogging:

"All free options have some limitations"

Beside the free platforms there are so many popular paid options available on internet. Like as a blogger I run my paid blog " http://blogratorcom " from a paid hosting service provider (Not from WordPress or Blogger or any free platform). A paid hosting service provider company provides different types of hosting options like WordPress Hosting, Panel Hosting (CPanel, Plesk Panel etc). As I told earlier that the open source popular CMS web applications like WordPress and Joomla can be installed on a web server. So if you buy a panel hosting from a web hosting service provider then you can install a open source application on your server and start blogging. The WordPress hosting are basically costly than panel hosting. Panel hosting means freedom to any web designer/ developer. Only WordPress hosting is totally different from panel hosting.

You can use WordPress application to run your blog in panel hosting but with WordPress hosting you got no access to panel.

How to make money from blogging?

I already described in my above writing about how to make money from blogging. Here I am giving more info about it. So you already know from the writing there are only two basic ways to make money from blogging. First and most popular one is Affiliate Marketing and second one is Google Adsense.

You can make money from affiliate marketing but not from Google AdSense if you are using free blog/website in WordPress. But you can earn from both if you are blogging for free from Blogger platform.

There are two basic ways to make money from a blog. First and most effective one is affiliate marketing and second one is Google AdSense.

Sounds familiar and easy? No, it's not that easy to make money from a blog as it sounds. Whether it is affiliate marketing or Google AdSense you will need good traffic in your website/blog.

But how to get the traffic?

Traffic can be got in two ways organic and inorganic. Organic traffic is when your articles are visible in the search engines and the visitors are reaching your blog through the search results. The inorganic traffic can be got in two ways paid promotions and social media sharing.

It is the raw materials of your blog (called contents) that attracts the search engines to give you the organic traffic. Organic traffic is very important because you don't have to pay for the traffic. But besides adding good contents in your blog you should know little technical skills called SEO.

What are the basics of SEO?

1. Whether you have added your free/paid blog/website as property in Google Analytics.

2. Whether you have confirmed your property in Google Search Console (webmasters tools).

3. Whether you know how to use Google Search Console (webmasters tools)?

4. Whether you have submitted your sitemap to Google.

5. Whether you have requested Google for indexing and render for both www and non www versions, mobile and desktop versions, http and https versions.

6. Have you confirmed whether you want www or non www version to be visible in Google search engine?

7. Have you selected your targeted country?

8. Have you used language tag in your every blog posts?

9. Whether you know about Keywords and content writing strategy.

So if you can create (or hire content writers for) great SEO friendly contents then only the contents are not enough to give you good organic traffic. Now I will discuss about some paid promotions.

What are the paid promotions?

1. Google Adwords and bing ads.
2. Social Media Advertisements.
3. Email Marketing.

You can also get traffics in your blog if you promote your entire blog or blog posts in search engines like google.com and bing.com through Google Adwords and Bing Ads like platforms. Then your blog or the articles will be visible at the top or bottom for some related search results (you can set the keywords at adwords). Also you can geographically target your audience. The traffics you get from the Search Engine Advertisements (SEA) are called paid inorganic traffic.

Social media advertisements are another way to get inorganic traffic in your blog. You may have seen in your facebook page there are boost options for every single post. Like that from twitter, linkedin, tumblr, instagram etc you can promote or boost your posts/tweets to hundreds, thousands of people geographically by paying some money (depends) to the platform.

Now comes email marketing. It is the spacial weapon that every blogger should give their full attention. Its not easy to grow subscription list by email. Experience and proper planning can help you grow your email list.

Why email list is very important for any blogger?

Growing email list is not only important for the bloggers but also companies. When a visitor subscribes your blog by email then the visitor will be notified by mail for every single post you publish after that. So from one side it is free promotion that brings back your old visitor again and again and that is the best promotion for your blog. But when you will grow huge subscribers list then it won't be free anymore. If you use free emails like gmail, yahoo, outlook etc then the free mails have daily or monthly or hourly limitations for sending mail. So you can't use your free mail to sent bulk mails to your subscribers. In that case you will need some professional platforms to send bulk mails. Those platforms charge some money depending on monthly limits.

Why you need a professional email address to send new post notifications from your website?

If you don't know what is a professional mail then here is an example, mail@blogrator.com this is a professional mail for my registered domain blogrator.com

If you are thinking to send new post notifications with your free email then you never can win your customer's trust. The free emails have no standard if you are representing whether your blog or business.

Besides if you send new post notifications to your subscribers from a free email like gmail, outlook then the subscriber may not recognize the sender. Also the subscriber may think the mail as spam and then report and unsubscribe it from your mailing list. It will be a big lose. So a free mail is not a solution to send new post notification to your subscribers. You will need a professional mail.

How to get a professional mail?

To get professional mails you need to buy a domain name (e.g, blogrator.com) from a hosting company (if you haven't been already running your blog from your personal domain). If you are running a free blog then you can buy a similar like name of your blog. After purchasing a domain from a hosting company you can buy a professional mail of your domain name from there. Also google Suite provides you to get professional emails as many as you want in exchange of very little price.

I am describing here the steps how to do it:

Step 1: Buy a domain name from a hosting company.

Step 2: Create a professional mail from domain & hosting service provider or Google Suite.

Step 3: To send bulk mails to the subscribers (or to grow subscribers list) use bulk mail sending service.

Now I will be talking about the social sharing option to grow your audience (free inorganic traffic) in your blog.

What is social media sharing?

1. Sharing in the facebook page and timeline.
2. Sharing in twitter, Linkedin, Tumblr, Instagram like platforms.

3. Making videos for your brand YouTube Channel on the blog topics.
4. Writing answers in Quora and Yahoo answers like platforms.

Social media sharing is a very good option to get free inorganic traffic. I believe the social media platforms help to get traffic inside the platform. Like you may have seen that you get free likes followers and requests in your facebook, twitter or linkedin accounts. You need to create the accounts in social media with your blog/website name. And don't forget to link your social media pages with your blog. Whenever you publish a new article then share it with those pages as soon as possible.

This way you will get all round traffic in your blog and that will help you to get commission from the products you recommend whenever there will be a purchase. And also you will earn some commission from the AdSense for Content Program.

TEN

WHAT IS A SUB DOMAIN? HOW IS IT RELATED TO FREE BLOGS?

"A sub domain isn't always related to a free blog"

There are a few popular websites like WordPress, Blogspot, Joomla, Quora that provide limited free space to an user in a sub domain to use it like a website/blog.

For example: http://blogrator.com is a main website but http://in.blogrator.com is a sub domain of blogrator. Both the main and sub domain work as a normal website that one can't differentiate.

Normally only the owner of the main website can create a sub domain and use it or give access on it to somebody else. Giving a separate access in a sub domain to someone else is not easy without an web application installed on it. Here WordPress and Joomla do the job better as a web application installed on a sub domain for users.

Anybody who owns a website can create a sub domain to use it for different purpose or give access on it to a different person by installing wordpress, Joomla like CMS (Content Management System) application on it.

The problem is if you are not a pro programmer then you can't limit the space to the separate user by yourself. So if you give a sub domain of your website to someone else then you and the user or the users will use the same space and database that has been allocated for you. This problem can be solved if you use premium hosting plans.

Popular websites like WordPress, Blogspot, Joomla gives user the permission to open a free blog in a unique sub domain of the user's choice. Here the sub domains can be created by the users because the websites are programmed that way. It also limits the space to the user. If the user wants more space then the user needs to buy it from them. Also an user can buy a personal .com .org .edu etc like domains from them. I have seen those hosting options are little costly comparing to other popular web hosting options. Here is my recommendation for domain and hosting plan in budget.

WordPress and Joomla both are open source web based a CMS application those can be installed on a hosting space to create a website. CMS stands for Content Management System. Wordpress.org maintains WordPress and Joomla.org maintains joomla application. But if want to open your free blog with WordPress or Joomla then you have to go either WordPress.com or Joomla.com as you like. Also you can open a free blog at blogger.com to get a sub domain of blogspot.com .

"Blogger was developed by Pyra Labs, which was bought by Google in 2003. Generally, the blogs are hosted by Google at a subdomain of blogspot.com. Blogger cannot be installed on a web server."

ELEVEN

HOW TO CREATE AN E-COMMERCE WEBSITE?

It is very easy to create an eCommerce website without any coding skills. An eCommerce website is a platform from where you can upload your products or services. Also you can receive the customer orders and payments automatically.

What do you need to create an eCommerce store without any coding knowledge?

1. You will need a domain (website name),
2. WordPress hosting or panel hosting (WordPress hosting via panel).

Buy your domain and hosting from a good web hosting service provider.

Now there are two conditions:

Have you purchased **WordPress hosting** or **panel hosting**?

If you have panel hosting then you have to install WordPress application on your domain address. For example I have installed the WordPress application on the root folder of blogrator.com. Also you can install it in other folders like blogrator.com/store.

For **WordPress hosting users** the panel part is already done and you don't have access to the panel.

Here are the steps that you have to follow now:

1. Login to the WordPress dashboard as admin.
2. Now go to plugins.
3. Click on Add new.
4. Now search WooCommerce plugin and install it.

5. Go through the entire setting process that the plugin will take you automatically.

6. Set your payments details. (i.e, add paypal, Payoneer and other payments options to accept payments from customers.)

7. Now you need to install a eCommerce supporting theme. WooCommerce recommends to use free theme Storefront but as it look very basic so you can buy any premium good looking WooCommerce supported theme like WoodMart, XSTORE (see all the list of top eCommerce themes)

8. The plugin and supporting theme will take care of everything and all you need to know is "How to add a product in WordPress using WooCommerce plugin?"- very simple

9. If you don't have your own product or service to sell then you can make some profit using the eCommerce platform by affiliate products.

How to create affiliate store website using WooCommerce plugin?

Step 1:

Step 2:

Step 3:

That's it! You are good to go.

TWELVE

HOW TO CREATE PASSIVE INCOME BY SELF PUBLISHING BOOKS?

I have successfully created passive income source by self publishing books on Amazon, Fliplart and other platforms. Also both my paperback and ebooks are being sold worldwide. I have started writing this article after I sold more that 150 copies of my self published books combining from all the platforms in the year of 2021. I have mentioned here "what are the platforms I use to self publish my books?"

I will share all my experiences and challenges throughout this writing. I will also make sure that after reading this article you will get the full understanding about self publishing. And believe me anyone can do it. Also you need no money to self publish your book.

When I was planning to self publish my book for the first time then I had many unanswered questions in my mind. Hopefully I am here for you to clear all your doubts. I will give you step by step clear idea to do it successfully. All you have to do is to copy my technique.

Whether you are a pro writer or have no experience in writing you will be equally benefited after complete reading this article.

This is going to be a lengthy guide and will be broken into many posts so my advice is if you subscribe the newsletter then you will keep receiving the new updates related to my successful zero investment passive income sources in future.

Write your Book

You can simply start writing your book in MS Word. It is better to have knowledge in page size and margin setup in MS word. Because at the time of publishing you will have to choose a book size and your doc file's page size should be of the same size of the book size. Also you have to use the recommended margin of your word file.

For your reference, here I am giving you some recommend standard sizes in inches for different type of books,

- **Fiction**: 4.25 x 6.87, 5 x 8, 5.25 x 8, 5.5 x 8.5, 6 x 9
- **Novella**: 5 x 8
- **Children's**: 7.5 x 7.5, 7 x 10, 10 x 8
- **Textbooks**: 6 x 9, 7 x 10, 8.5 x 11
- **Non-fiction**: 5.5 x 8.5, 6 x 9, 7 x 10″

If you are planning to self publish your book for the first time then my advice is to start with a book of small number of pages. Do you know you can even publish a book with 10 pages only!

As you are self publishing the book all by yourself so your first few books will not be perfect and it is very common for all self publishers. But if you are very serious about perfectness then you have to hire professionals. You can very easily find professional freelances in freelancing platforms like fiverr, freelancer, upwork etc. I haven't hired any professional till now and I have sold 150+ books in the year of 2021. In 2022 I have taken a target of 500+ books to sell.

I do a full time job that is my mainstream income. Passive income for the first few years doesn't give a good earning. But some extra earning in every month is not bad right? And who knows in a few years your passive earning source won't become your mainstream income.

Earnings Report View Ledger

			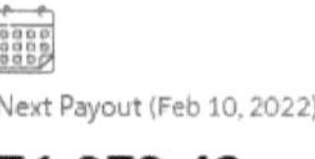
Lifetime Earnings	Total Books Sold	Pending Earnings	Next Payout (Feb 10, 2022)
₹10,055	**107**	**₹1,964.27**	**₹1,873.42**

My next month payout from this platform is 1873.42 INR.

Design Book Cover

Lets consider you have successfully written your book. So now you have to design the front and back cover for your book.

I am not a professional graphic designer but I design my book covers by myself.

I do all my graphic designing work from Canva,

Canva is free with limited usage. You may subscribe for paid if required. Or you can simply pay for premium photo if you want to use them. The paid photos only costs 1USD. I am using Canva since 2017 and almost in all graphic design I use free images.

Printed by Libri Plureos GmbH in Hamburg,
Germany